A PRACTICAL GUIDE TO THE
GIFT OF TONGUES

First published in 2010 by
by New Life Publishing, Luton,
Bedfordshire LU4 9HG

© John Vaughan-Neil

British Library Cataloguing in Publication Data
A catalogue record for this book is available
from the British Library

ISBN   978 1 903623 47 3

Unless otherwise indicated, all scripture
quotations are taken with permission from
the Jerusalem Bible, copyright 1966, 1967, 1968
by Darton Longman and Todd Limited
and Doubleday & Company Limited.

Typesetting by New Life Publishing,
Luton, UK   www.goodnewsbooks.net
Printed and bound in Great Britain

A PRACTICAL GUIDE TO THE
GIFT OF TONGUES

JOHN VAUGHAN-NEIL

To my wife, Mary,
whose selfless love,
all down the years,
has sustained us all

THE AUTHOR

JOHN VAUGHAN-NEIL is a Catholic, married with three daughters and lives in the parish of the Sacred Heart, Wimbledon. He was educated at the local Jesuit College and at University College Oxford, where he read law. As a Solicitor (now retired) he had a very varied career embracing private practice and public industry.

For 15 years he led one of the local prayer groups which 'dissolved' in 1995 to form evangelisation cell groups. In the mid 1980's he published a seminar programme on living in the power of the Holy Spirit entitled 'Sons and Daughters of the Living God' (which is published by New Life Publishing) and over recent years he has been in regular demand giving a one day programme in parishes on effective evangelisation, entitled 'Spread the Word!'. He is a regular speaker at national conferences, days of renewal and seminar programmes in the U.K. and abroad, and he has conducted workshops on the gift of tongues for the past 25 years.

ACKNOWLEDGMENTS

All italics in scripture extracts and
quotations from other authors have
been introduced by the author.

A model for running a workshop
on the gift of tongues is given
in the author's renewal programme
Sons and Daughters of the Living God
also published by New Life Publishing.

My special thanks to Fr. Pat Collins, C.M.
for his kindness in reading this guide
and for his very valuable suggestions.

CONTENTS

FOREWORD

THERE IS a saying that clear waters, like fountains, do not seem so deep as they really are. Although John Vaughan Neil's book is deceptively simple, succinct and practical, it is clearly the fruit of years of personal experience, profound reflection and wide reading.

It is aimed at those within and outside the Charismatic Renewal who want to know more about this intriguing gift. It explains the nature of praying and speaking in tongues from a biblical point of view and the motives Christians have for desiring this ability, while proposing practical means of yielding to, and exercising it.

The Vatican II Constitution on the Church says in para.12 that charisms, such as tongues, "are to be received with thanksgiving and consolation for they are perfectly suited to and useful for the needs of the Church." I am confident that this excellent guide will enable its many readers to respond in a positive way to the Council's recommendation.

Pat Collins, C.M.

INTRODUCTION

First encounter

MY FIRST encounter with people exercising the gift of tongues was at a charismatic weekend conference in Roehampton, London in September 1978. It was organised by the Family of God Prayer Group founded in the early 1970s by Tim and Mimi Turner, who were amongst the earliest leaders in the renewal in this country. At the time, I had the advantage of having read a little about this gift and had even asked the Holy Spirit to help me to yield to Him in the gift of tongues. Nevertheless, I was understandably slightly stunned by the live experience. When many of those assembled began to sing in tongues, I found myself instinctively looking up and wondering if we had been joined by a choir of angels...the exquisite beauty of this hymn of praise seemed to belong to a realm beyond this world. Little did I know that, not long afterwards, at the time of my baptism in the Spirit, I myself would experience the enormous blessing of yielding to this gift.

Subsequently - after I was asked to take a share in the leadership of the Family of God Prayer Group - I learnt just how important it is to give in-depth teaching on this gift if we are to help people yield to it and also to help everyone use it to its full potential. That is what I have been doing in workshops on the gift of tongues for the past twenty-five years.

We Christians do not know who we really are!

St. Paul is so emphatic when writing to the Corinthians that they should not be ignorant of the gifts: "Now brothers, I do not want you to be ignorant about the spiritual gifts." (1Cor.12:1) One of the saddest features of our life in the Church to-day, however, is that so many Christians in the mainstream Christian Churches *are* very ignorant about the gifts of the Holy Spirit.

In his book 'A New Pentecost?' Cardinal Suenens puts this most tellingly:

"What is lacking in us is a realisation of our Christian identity. We dare not believe with an expectant faith that the various gifts of the Spirit are always there for the Church of God. We do not recall often enough that we are rich with the riches of God.....

We Christians do not know who we are. We are children of God, heirs to his Kingdom, *but we behave as if it were not so.* We have at our disposal spiritual treasures which remain buried because their existence is unknown to us, or because we lack the faith to believe that they can be found and used."

This guide is a small contribution to remedying this situation, at least as far as the gift of tongues is concerned.

Who is this guide for and what does it cover?

This guide is not meant to be in any way an academic or exhaustive treatment of the subject. It is intended to be a simple, practical guide written for:

- those who are attending Life in the Spirit seminars;
- those who have experienced baptism in the Holy Spirit but have not yet yielded to this gift;
- those who have already experienced the manifestation of this gift but who may not feel confident in exercising it, or have sadly abandoned the use of it;
- those who do exercise this gift but have received little in the way of teaching about it.

and designed to give a clear understanding of:

- exactly what this gift is;
- the many wonderful purposes that it serves;
- how to open ourselves to the Holy Spirit so
  we can yield to this gift under His prompting; and
- how to grow in the use of this gift.

The appendices

There are quite a number of matters on which, for the
sake of completeness, I think it would be appropriate
to give some help in this guide, but which would be
distracting if included in the main text. These I have
dealt with in the appendices.

Solid teaching and practical help

This short guide has been written with two overall
groups in mind. The first comprises those who have
had no experience of the gift of tongues. The second
comprises those who have already yielded to the
gift, but have never been given anything like a full
understanding of the scope of it, or been encouraged
to harness its phenomenal power. They have been
left, we might say, just to 'get on with it.' As a

consequence, many are stuck in 'first gear' and the gift remains seriously underused. They are in sore need of a truly refreshing *boost*, which I hope this guide will give them.

Both these groups need solid teaching and practical help, which I have sought to provide in these pages. And it is my deepest hope that the Holy Spirit will use this guide to help everyone mature in the fullest possible way both in, and through, this most powerful and precious gift of prayer.

ONE

WHAT EXACTLY *IS* THE GIFT OF TONGUES?

I T SEEMS best to begin by describing exactly what *is* the gift of tongues. Tongues is a very powerful form of prayer in which you allow the Holy Spirit to pray aloud in you. You will appreciate just how powerful this prayer is when we consider in Chapter 4 the purposes it serves and the fruit that it brings. For the moment, however, let me summarise the essential features of this form of prayer, as follows:

• When you pray in tongues, you use your normal voice to speak out, but what you are saying is given to you by the Holy Spirit. You are not speaking any known, human language, but in a special language of the Spirit *that is unique to you*. No two people praying in tongues pray in exactly the same way.

• When the Holy Spirit prays in you in this way, your intellect is not involved in composing what you are saying. You simply allow the language of the Spirit to flow from your lips. Generally, it has some kind of linguistic form, a particular pattern, but it is expressed in syllables and sounds rather than what we would identify as 'words'.

- Normally, we neither understand, nor have any need to understand, what we are saying when we pray in tongues. The syllables and sounds we utter have no conceptual meaning.

- On rare occasions, however, we may be given an interpretation of what has been said when we are praying in tongues, through the exercise of the gift of interpretation. Furthermore, many people praying in tongues have occasionally experienced the Spirit praying in them in a language that is a known language - Portuguese, Russian or whatever. But I must emphasise: *this is not the norm!* Such an experience is a 'one –off ' through which the Holy Spirit wishes to touch the heart of someone who is listening nearby and who happens to speak that same language. The person praying in these situations has no idea what they them- selves are actually saying as they speak in a foreign language.

One of the most dramatic examples of this that the American evangelist Don Basham recounts arose at a prayer meeting held on a university campus. On one occasion at which all those present were praying in the Spirit, one of the group (not one of the musicians) took up a drum and began to beat it rhythmically and very loudly. A few minutes later, a student entered the room and enquired who had been using his tribal drum language. Apparently the drummer had been beating out a message of the love of Jesus, speaking to the very heart of the newcomer who at the time had been two floors up!

There have also been wonderful examples down the centuries of evangelists being anointed by the Spirit to speak in native languages that they had never learnt. St.Vincent Ferrer and St.Francis Xavier are just two examples. There have also been instances of evangelists speaking *only* in their own native language and their hearers understanding them in their (different) languages. However, as emphasised above, such experiences are not encountered in the normal, day-to-day, exercise of the gift.

• Tongues does not *displace* praying in our own native language, nor does it in any way render it 'second rate'. Rather, it is a gift that *supplements* our normal prayer and comes into its own when ordinary human language begins to fail us, or fails us completely.

• Although praying in tongues is exhilarating, it is not an ecstatic experience, and there is no question of the Holy Spirit taking over control of our speech.

• The exercise of this gift remains entirely under our personal control. Once you have yielded to this gift, you can thereafter pray in tongues whenever you wish to do so, starting and stopping when you so choose.

• Finally, the actual experience of yielding to the gift of tongues is something *very* simple: much simpler than you might otherwise expect.

TWO

HOW DOES THE HOLY SPIRIT WORK THROUGH HIS GIFTS?

A fundamental misunderstanding

REGRETTABLY, it is my experience that the way in which the Holy Spirit actually works in us through His gifts is widely misunderstood. I should like to address this matter at the outset, therefore, so the gift of tongues can be properly understood against the backdrop of how the gifts work generally.

The particular misunderstanding to which I refer, and to which many are prone, is the idea that the gifts are either things that we *have*, or more often than not, things we have *not yet got*, but which the Holy Spirit might someday give us, if we are fortunate! This is a wholly distorted image of the gifts and how the Holy Spirit works through them.

We 'have' no gifts!

In the early 1970s Cardinal Suenens was appointed
by Pope Paul V1 to examine and report to him on the
spread of charismatic renewal which millions of
Catholics had begun to experience at that time. The
Cardinal subsequently wrote what must be one of
the most important books ever written on the
renewal, entitled 'A New Pentecost?' (latterly
published by Fiat under the title 'The Holy Spirit –
Life Breath of the Church Volume 1'). In it, he
addressed this fundamental misunderstanding
concerning the gifts and his teaching can be summed
up as follows:

• The gifts of the Spirit are the ways in which the
Holy Spirit works in us.
• The gifts are not *things* that we *possess*: they can
only belong to the Holy Spirit - just as the rays of the
sun belong only to the sun.
• We, therefore, *do not 'have' any gifts at all!* But
what we *do* have is the Holy Spirit Himself. When I
receive Him, I receive the fullness of all that is His –
including all His gifts!
• This does not mean that the gifts, which belong to
the Spirit, will all be manifested in me, nor that they
will be manifested in me in the same way or at the
same time.
• The ways in which the Holy Spirit works in us
will differ not only from person to person, but also

in each individual, according to the degree of faith, hope and love He finds in us and also according to whatever work the Father entrusts to us. To-day's work will require certain gifts: tomorrow's work may require other, different, gifts. In each case, we can rely upon the Holy Spirit to manifest the gifts that are needed for the task – either in me personally or collectively in the community.

• The way the Holy Spirit may manifest His gifts in me is entirely unlimited. Depending on what the Father is doing through me, the Holy Spirit may manifest in me *not just one gift, but many, either successively or all at once.*

• We must always keep in mind that the Holy Spirit does not work within some kind of rigid framework, but moves among us with supreme freedom.

Liberated to move in the power of the Spirit

In the teaching outlined above, Cardinal Suenens is not playing around with language. The various points he makes are *extremely* important for us to understand so we are truly free to move in the power and love of the Holy Spirit. Furthermore, they are entirely in accordance with the experience of the disciples as recorded in Acts and indeed with the experience of the apostles and disciples commissioned by Jesus when He sent out the twelve and the seventy-two. Nobody in Acts is described as 'owning' any gifts. The early Christian communities simply delighted in the great works wrought by the Holy Spirit as they went about their business of proclaiming the gospel.

Suenens shows us how misguided it is to be focussed on the gifts rather than the Holy Spirit Himself, who empowers us to carry out whatever work the Father is calling us to do at any particular moment. *It is the job that counts: the gifts become operative with the job.* If we fall into the way of thinking and speaking of the gifts as things we are *given* and which then *belong* to us, we severely undermine our openness to the action of the Holy Spirit and restrict the freedom that He requires to work in us.

Tools for the job

A toolbox can be a useful analogy to reinforce Suenens' teaching (although we must remember that the gifts are not *'things'*!) The gifts are like tools in a toolbox. The tools belong to the Holy Spirit who uses whatever tools are necessary for the job we have been given at any particular time, working through us individually or collectively.

Seeing the gifts in the light of this analogy emphasises just how important it is to focus on the Holy Spirit, *discerning what the job is*, and to recognise that all the tools required for it are brought into use by the working of the Holy Spirit. It also serves to illustrate just how debilitating it is for us to think that any of the tools actually *belong* to us and (as a result) that we only 'have' the tools that we have used to date. That is like going around saying to ourselves: "Great! I've got a screwdriver! But I've not yet got a hammer! So, for the time being, Lord, I will only be on the lookout for jobs which require a screwdriver!" when all along there is a complete toolbox at the Spirit's disposal.

A cautionary tale

I am reminded of an embarrassing incident in the early years of our local prayer group, which may serve as a cautionary tale. One evening the service team asked a visiting priest to pray for a lady in the group who was ill and we gathered with her for this purpose in the chapel. After praying for a while, the priest turned round to us and said: "Has anyone got a word of knowledge?" I am ashamed to say that we just looked at him, and each other, in stark amazement. His question had taken us by surprise, betraying our classic misunderstanding of how the Holy Spirit works. We thought it was a gift which none of us had'!! As a result, we presumed that it was the priest alone who was going to be exercising all the gifts necessary to minister to this woman and our part would be just to pray generally in support of him.

What we had utterly failed to appreciate was that, although the Holy spirit had not manifested the gift of knowledge in any of us prior to that evening, the priest was quite rightly expecting us to be totally open to however the Holy Spirit might wish to move amongst us. In particular, the priest was keen that all of us should be open to receiving any word of knowledge the Spirit might wish to bring to our minds concerning the woman for whom we were praying. The fact that the Holy Spirit had not manifested this gift in us previously was, therefore, totally irrelevant. We were now acting on the prompting of the Holy spirit to pray for this woman's healing and we needed to be alert to whatever gifts He might manifest amongst us in order to heal her.

Come Holy Spirit!

"Be filled with the Spirit." (Ephesians 5:18)

The Holy Spirit continually pours Himself out upon us in all His fullness - a point that is emphasised in the more literal translation of the above text, which in the Greek reads: "*Keep being* filled with the Spirit." So whenever we pray: 'Come holy Spirit!", we are in effect asking the Holy Spirit not so much 'to come' (as if He were somehow absent), but to help us - 'to come *to our aid*'- in particular with a fresh outpouring upon us – and to open our hearts more fully to receive all that He brings us. This plea does not reflect our 'losing' the power of the Holy Spirit - as if we were a 'leaking tank' – but rather our need to increase our desire and willingness to embrace Him – for which, if you like, we need our tank *enlarging*!

As to the Spirit's gifts, Paul encourages us *to desire and to hope* for their manifestation. This means essentially to ask the Holy Spirit to fill our hearts with expectation, to increase our faith, our hope and our love and to quicken our hearts to discern and follow all His promptings as He shows us the Father's will. For it is only doing the Father's will that matters and to which all our energies should be directed, as Jesus Himself reminds us:

"It is not those who say to me, 'Lord, Lord', who will enter the kingdom of heaven, but the person who does the will of my Father in heaven. When the day comes, many will say to me: 'Lord, Lord, did we not prophesy in your name, cast out demons in your name, work many miracles in your name?' Then I shall tell them to their faces: I have never known you; away from me you evil men!" (Mt.7:21-23)

THREE

WHAT DOES SCRIPTURE TELL US ABOUT THE GIFT OF TONGUES?

TO DEEPEN our understanding of the gift of tongues, and to welcome and co-operate with the Holy Spirit's desire to pray in us, we now need to look at what Scripture tells us about this gift.

Jesus' teaching in Mark

"These are the signs that will be associated with believers: in my name they will cast out devils; they will have the gift of tongues; and they will pick up snakes in their hands, and be unharmed should they drink deadly poison; they will lay their hands on the sick, who will recover." (Mark 16:17-18)

It may come as a surprise to some that the first mention we have in scripture of the gift of tongues is contained in this statement by Jesus given at the very end of St.Mark's gospel. It highlights two very important aspects of the gift.

First, it is highly significant that, of the numerous

gifts which the Holy Spirit would in due course manifest among his followers, Jesus draws *special attention* here to just *three* of them: deliverance from evil spirits, and the gifts of tongues and healing.

The disciples had personally witnessed Jesus exercising two of these gifts on countless occasions - deliverance and healing. Furthermore, the same two gifts had marked the missions of the apostles and of the seventy-two disciples themselves (see Luke 9:1-6 and Luke 10: 1-24).

As to the gift of tongues, Jesus Himself will undoubtedly have prayed in tongues, so it is possible that His disciples may have previously received some teaching from Him about this gift, as well as actually witnessing it when they were at prayer with Him. However, whether it was new to them or not, it is striking that Jesus now singles out the gift of tongues, alongside deliverance and healing.

Upon reflection, the obvious conclusion as to why He did this is that, *just as these three gifts were central to Jesus' own life and ministry, so they would become central to the lives and ministry of His followers.*

Second, Jesus tells us that the gift of tongues is to be associated with His followers *generally* - *not* just a minority of a particularly zealous or extravert disposition!

Tongues is the first gift manifest at Pentecost

"When Pentecost day came round, they had all met in one room, when suddenly they heard what sounded like a powerful wind from heaven, the noise of which filled the entire house in which they were sitting; and something appeared to them that seemed like tongues of fire; these separated and came to rest on the head of each of them. They were all filled with the Holy Spirit, and *began to speak with foreign languages as the Spirit gave them the gift of speech.*"

It so happens that when the Holy Spirit came on those gathered in the upper room at Pentecost, the gift of tongues was the first gift of the Spirit to be manifest! Furthermore, the account tells us that the gift was manifest in *everyone* there - all the apostles and all the disciples and, of course, Our Lady in their midst.

The Holy Spirit manifested other gifts, too, very quickly indeed, including the gifts of fortitude and preaching, in which the disciples were emboldened to take to the streets and preach to the large crowd, together with the gift of prophecy, through which they proclaimed the wonders that God had worked. But it is significant that the first gift manifest was the gift of tongues.

Further events in the Acts of the Apostles

There are four other occasions recorded in Acts of the initial outpouring of the Holy Spirit on those who became believers in Jesus.

Peter and John pray over the Samaritans

The first occasion is when the Samaritans come to accept the gospel and Peter and John go down to pray over them because they had not as yet received the Holy Spirit:

"When the apostles in Jerusalem heard that Samaria had accepted the word of God, they sent Peter and John to them, and they went down there and prayed for the Samaritans to receive the Holy Spirit, for as yet he had not come down on any of them: they had only been baptised in the name of the Lord Jesus. Then they laid hands on them and they received the Holy Spirit." (Acts 8:14-16)

Following this event, an unfortunate incident is recorded (see verses 17-24) in which a magician by the name of Simon, who had recently renounced his black arts and become a believer, witnesses this outpouring of the Holy Spirit on the Samaritans and offers Peter some money so that the Holy Spirit will come on others when *he* lays *his* hands on them! Peter gives Simon a severe rebuke for thinking that he can buy the power to confer the gift of the Holy Spirit.

What is so interesting about this part of the story is that Simon has quite clearly *seen something happening* to the Samaritan disciples when Peter and John laid hands on them for the outpouring of the Holy Spirit. Otherwise, how would he have known that the Samaritans had received the Holy Spirit and what reason would he have had to try and buy the power if it had not been visibly demonstrated through Peter and John?

Peter preaches to Cornelius and his household
Exactly *what* Simon has seen and heard is not left to our imagination for very long because two chapters later, Luke *expressly* records what happens when Peter preaches for the first time to the Gentiles.

"While Peter was still speaking the Holy Spirit came

down on all the listeners. Jewish believers who
had accompanied Peter were all astonished that
the gift of the Holy Spirit should be poured out
on the pagans too, since they could hear them
speaking in tongues and proclaiming the greatness of
God. Peter himself then said: 'Could anyone refuse
the water of baptism to these people, *now they have*
received the Holy Spirit just as much as we have?' He
then gave orders for them to be baptised in the name
of Jesus Christ. Afterwards they begged him to stay
on for some days." (Acts 10: 44 - 48)

It is a reasonable assumption that what Paul
witnessed here with Cornelius is precisely what
Simon had witnessed in the earlier incident
recorded in Acts Chapter 8.

Paul prays over John's disciples at Ephesus

When we come to the account of Paul meeting some
disciples at Ephesus, we again find the Holy Spirit
manifesting the very same gifts in those experiencing
the initial outpouring of the Holy Spirit:

"While Apollos was in Corinth, Paul made his way
overland as far as Ephesus, where he found a
number of disciples. When he asked: 'Did you
receive the Holy Spirit when you became believers?'
they answered, 'No. We were never even told there

was such a thing as a Holy Spirit.' 'Then how were you baptised?' he asked. 'With John's baptism' they replied. 'John's baptism,' said Paul, 'was a baptism of repentance; but he insisted that the people should believe in the one who was to come after him – in other words Jesus.' When they heard this, they were baptised in the name of the Lord Jesus and the moment Paul had laid hands on them the Holy Spirit came down on them, *and they began to speak with tongues and to prophesy.* There were about twelve of these men." (Acts 19: 1 - 7)

Note here that the phrase *'and to prophesy'* would mean that they were also moved by the Holy Spirit to 'proclaim the greatness of God' – in exactly the same way as was experienced at Pentecost, in the house of Cornelius, and (by implication) when Peter and John prayed over the Samaritans.

The conversion of Saul

The one further occasion recorded in Acts of the initial outpouring of the Holy Spirit on believers is when Jesus sends Ananias to pray over Saul so that he may recover his sight and be filled with the Holy Spirit. (Acts 9: 10-19) On that occasion there is no mention of the gifts of tongues and prophecy, but given all the other examples we have considered, it must be at the very least probable that the Holy Spirit manifested these same gifts as soon as Ananias had prayed over him. We do know from his first letter to the Corinthians that Paul used the gift of tongues extensively, where he says in an aside: 'I pray in the Spirit with thanksgiving: I pray in tongues more than all of you.' (1 Cor.14 v.18 *Author*)

What are we to conclude from scripture?

The foregoing accounts are the only instances of the initial outpouring of the Holy Spirit described in Acts. In view of their consistency it seems reasonable to suppose that exercising the gift of tongues must have been *the norm* for the early Christians. This conclusion is even more robust when we realise that Paul devoted the whole of chapter 14 of his first letter to the Corinthians on the use of the gift of tongues in public worship. The difficulty he was addressing was that the whole church in Corinth was using the gift of tongues when they gathered for public worship but neglecting the gift of prophecy to the detriment of non-believers.

There are two further conclusions that can be reasonably drawn from Scripture. First, because the accounts in Acts expressly record with such regularity the manifestation of the gift of tongues (together, as it happens, with prophecy), the gift of tongues is a *very important* gift and particularly so, given the way Jesus singles it out at the end of Mark's gospel. Second, it should not escape our notice that where the gift of tongues is mentioned in Acts, it is recorded that *everyone* prayed in tongues. This underpins my understanding that this is a gift which is *available to all believers*.

FOUR

BUT WHAT'S THE *PURPOSE* OF IT?

Power to evangelise

"...but you will receive power when the Holy Spirit comes on you and then you will be my witnesses... to the ends of the earth."(Acts 1:8)

" 'And now Lord, take note of their threats and help your servants to *proclaim your message with all boldness,* by stretching out your hand to heal and to work miracles and marvels through the name of your holy servant, Jesus.' As they prayed, the house where they were assembled rocked; they were all filled with the Holy Spirit and *began to proclaim the word of God boldly."* (Acts 4:29-31)

WE MUST always keep in mind the fact that the Holy Spirit has been poured out on us *to empower us to proclaim the Good News.* The gift of tongues, therefore, like all the gifts of the Holy Spirit, is one of the ways in which the Spirit empowers us to fulfil our calling to evangelise, to build the Kingdom of God. As Pope Paul V1 proclaimed in paragraph 13 of his magnificent encyclical Evangelii Nuntiandi ('Evangelisation in the Modern World'): "The Church exists in order to evangelise!" That is the reason we belong to the Church.

Of course, as Pope Paul goes on to say in that same paragraph 13, we prize all the sacramental life of the Church through which the Holy Spirit enables us to grow in holiness, upon which to a large degree the effectiveness of our evangelisation will depend. And we are repeatedly reminded of this dual purpose of the gift of the Holy Spirit when we pray in Eucharistic Prayer 1V:

"And that we might live no longer for ourselves but for him, he sent the Holy Spirit from you, Father, as his first gift to those who believe, to complete his work on earth (i.e. to evangelise) and bring us the fullness of grace (i.e. to be transformed in holiness)."

But we all need to be alive to the fact that *our job is to evangelise* and the gift of tongues is *an extremely powerful tool for the job*!

So let us now look at the spectacular array of purposes, within the overall context of our call to holiness and our call to evangelise, to which the Holy Spirit puts this great gift.

"Cry out with joy to the Lord, all the earth.
Serve the Lord with gladness.
Come before him, singing for joy.

Go within his gates, giving thanks.
Enter his courts with songs of praise.
Give thanks to him and bless his name."
(Psalm 99 v 1,2 & 4 Grail)

"Bring an offering and enter his courts,
worship the Lord in his temple.
O earth, tremble before him."
(Psalm 95: 8-9 Grail)

The fact is that the gift of tongues encompasses the expression of the entire range of our response to 'the love of God poured out in our hearts' – expressed from the very depths of our being. We cry aloud in praise and worship, joy and thanksgiving. All are bound up in our prayer as the body of Christ, all joined with His prayer to the Father.

It may be helpful, however, to gain an appreciation of the power of the gift of tongues to reflect on some of those aspects individually, beginning with praise.

Prayer of praise

Praise – which leads us into worship - is a most important aspect of the gift of tongues. We are made in the very image of God. We are made for Him - to know Him, to love Him and to serve Him, and to be with Him forever in heaven. When we are drawn by the Spirit into deep repentance and conversion and come to know the love of God, we enter into a deep, personal relationship of love with God and our whole being wants to cry out to Him in praise and to worship Him. However, our ordinary human language proves totally inadequate to express what is welling up within us and it is as if the Lord is saying to us: 'I know what you want to say and how your heart is reaching out to mine, but it is beyond all human words. Allow the Holy Spirit within you to express it - He will give you the word of praise to cry out from the very depths of your being and express the worship which is welling up in your heart.'

Praise in tongues, then, is our language of love responding to the love of God, responding to Him *simply for who He is* and expressing our deepest yearning to know Him fully. You could without exaggeration describe tongues as the language of paradise, of that most intimate communion that we all lost in the Fall, and which the Holy spirit now restores to us.

Prayer of thanksgiving

"Be happy at all times; pray constantly; *and for all things give thanks to God*, because this is what God expects you to do in Christ Jesus." (I Thess.5: 16-18)

"Go on singing and chanting to the Lord in your hearts so that *always and everywhere you are giving thanks* to God who is our Father in the name of the Lord Jesus Christ." (Eph.5:20)

Closely allied with praise is our prayer of thanksgiving, and as with praise, we soon find our human language fails to give anything approaching the full expression of thanksgiving that we wish to offer the Lord.

The above verses from 1 Thessalonians and Ephesians illustrate just how Paul's prayer life was centred on thanksgiving and how important it is that we follow his example. The same emphasis is found in his wonderful remark in 1 Cor.14: 18 which is invariably mistranslated as: "I thank God *that* I pray in tongues more than all of you."

Can you imagine saying to a group of people: "I thank God that I pray the rosary more than all of you!"? As we might expect, closer examination of the Greek text shows that Paul is not saying anything so bizarre and inappropriate. What he in fact says is: "I offer thanksgiving to God *(i.e. by praying in tongues)*: I pray in tongues more than all of you *put together!*"

In this little aside, Paul demonstrates the power of the gift of tongues. His exhortation to be 'always giving thanks' obviously reflected his own extensive use of the gift of tongues, which itself must have undoubtedly accounted in no small measure for the enormous power of his ministry.

Prayer of joy and exultation

"My soul proclaims the greatness of the Lord, and my spirit *exults* in God my saviour!" (Luke 1:46-47)

This marvellous outburst of joy begins the famous Magnificat. Our Lady was inspired to utter this prayer as she greeted her cousin Elizabeth at the Visitation, and it goes on in prophetic mode to proclaim the great things God has done for us - just as the disciples did at Pentecost.

And an easy parallel can be drawn between the Magnificat and the power of the gift of tongues to capture our own deepest joy in the Lord. The Holy Spirit praying in us in tongues could be said to give each of us our own unique magnificat, a magnificat of the Holy Spirit Himself, praying through us!

Prayer that builds us up

"He who speaks in a tongue edifies himself." (1 Cor.14:4)

"But you, my dear friends, must use your most holy faith as your foundation, and build on that, praying in the Holy Spirit." (Jude v 20)

"Out of his infinite glory, *may he give you the power through his Spirit* for your hidden self to grow strong, so that Christ may live in your hearts through faith, and then, planted in love and built on love, you will with all the saints have strength to grasp the breadth and the length, the height and the depth; until knowing the love of Christ, which is beyond all knowledge, you are filled with the utter fullness of God."

"Glory be to him *whose power, working in us, can do infinitely more than we can ask or imagine*; glory be to him from generation to generation in the Church and in Christ Jesus for ever and ever. Amen." (Eph.3: 16-21)

As indeed with any language of love, so the fruit of entering into this prayer of praise and thanksgiving in tongues is the building up of our relationship of love with the Father, the Son and the Holy Spirit Himself, and the strengthening of our faith. But more needs to be said on this because this 'edifying' and this 'building up', worked by the Spirit in power through the use of the gift of tongues, is *monumental*! Our whole spiritual development, the ultimate goal of which is 'to be filled with the utter fullness of God', is entirely the working of the Holy Spirit in us in power which we can tap into by using the gift of tongues. While we are praying in tongues for our own needs, the Holy Spirit is raising up *all* our needs - which He understands far better than we ever could – and all according to the heart and will of the Father.

This 'building up', therefore, covers so many concrete aspects of our spiritual growth there are too many to identify here, but we should at least note some of them. They include our need :

- to be led into all truth;
- to drink deeply of the Spirit welling up inside us so we proclaim the gospel with renewed zeal and power, and allow the spring of the Spirit to flow out and touch all those with whom we come into contact;
- for wisdom, discernment and guidance and to know God's will for us;
- to be alert to, recognise and respond to the prompting of the Holy Spirit;
- to constantly renew our purpose in Christ, our determination to follow Him in obedience;
- to respond to all the graces which the Lord pours out on us to fulfil our calling and to meet all the challenges we face; and
- to join our sufferings with those of Christ.

Prayer of petition and intercession

"The Spirit too comes to help us in our weakness. For when we cannot choose words in order to pray properly, *the Spirit Himself expresses our plea in a way that could never be put into words* (i.e. through our praying in tongues) and God who knows everything in our hearts, knows perfectly well what he (i.e. the Spirit) means, and that *the pleas of the saints expressed by the Spirit* (i.e. our petitions and intercession raised up using the gift of tongues) *are according to the mind of God.*" (Romans 8: 26-27)

The last phrase in this passage reads in the Greek: *'are according to God'* which is variously translated as according to 'the mind', 'the heart' or 'the will' of God.

In this marvellous passage, Paul explains how - when we pray in tongues - the Holy Spirit raises up to the Father those pleas of ours which are too deep to be expressed in human language. How many of us, from time to time, find ourselves lost for words in prayer when we are deeply burdened, or when we are assailed with problems too complex to analyse or express! Here in Romans, Paul explains just how wonderfully the gift of tongues comes to our rescue in crying out to God, with the Spirit Himself raising up our needs - not only in a way that is perfectly understood by the Father, but *according to the Father's heart and will!* When we are overwhelmed by life's troubles, what greater gift of prayer could we be offered than *that?*! In our use of tongues, too, we will experience the Holy Spirit upholding us in the midst of personal crisis – restoring and maintaining our peace of heart.

The gift of tongues, therefore, is a most powerful

means of raising up our own needs and the needs of others. The Holy Spirit in His wisdom knows our deepest needs much better than we do. In tongues He is praying, not merely for the needs we can see, but also our needs 'according to the Father's mind' - as seen by the Father! We might be praying, for example, for the healing of some physical sickness, whereas in addition the Holy Spirit may be praying for the healing of our refusal to forgive someone who has hurt us deeply.

When it comes to prayer of intercession, which by its very nature is very sustained and persistent, the gift of tongues also comes especially to our aid. While the general scope of the need for which we are pray-ing will be articulated at the outset in our native language (e.g. 'for the conversion of our country') its full ramifications are quite beyond us and tongues enables us to sustain our prayer at great length (hours at a time) in a way that does not tax us mentally or weary us physically in the way that praying in our native language would. For my own part, when praying by way of intercession I pray in tongues *softly under my breath* in a way that becomes as easy as breathing itself.

Weapon against temptation

"On the lips of children and of babes
you have found praise to foil your enemy,
to silence the foe and the rebel."
(Psalm 8:3 Grail)

"Finally, grow strong in the Lord, *with the strength of his power.* ...For it is not against human enemies that we have to struggle, but against the Sovereignties and the Powers who originate the darkness in this world, the spiritual army of evil in the heavens... So *stand your ground*... with all prayer and supplication, *pray at every opportunity in the Spirit.*" (Ephesians 4:10,12,14 & (NAB) 18)

With the gift of tongues we are specially armed for spiritual warfare *"with the strength of his power!"* It is in the context of spiritual warfare, immediately after describing the armour of God that we are to put on (in verses 14-17), that Paul exhorts us to stand our ground with all prayer and supplication and to *'pray at every opportunity in the Spirit.'* (It should be noted here that the phrase 'in the Spirit' means 'in tongues' – the Greek being identical to Paul's reference to praying in tongues in 1 Cor.14:16.)

Again, we have Paul emphasising the need for all of

us to follow his example and use our gift of tongues *constantly* – *'at every opportunity'* – not least in meeting and warding off temptation. We will always be encountering temptation through satan and his followers, the world and the flesh, and in the gift of tongues we have been given a most powerful weapon to deal with it.

The reason why tongues is such a powerful gift in this respect is quite simple. When we pray in the Spirit, He not only takes up our cry for help, but He raises us up in spirit in an intimate dialogue of love with the Father and Jesus. In their company we are immediately focussed away from our temptation and become fully open to the source of our strength to resist it. And as we respond to the grace then poured out on us, our temptations have to give way; they no longer have any place in us. They are choked off, so to speak - deprived of the very air they need for survival. They can no longer maintain any foothold in our heart or mind. And as we learn to use this weapon to greater and greater effect, we will find that we are falling less and less into sin.

Speaking on this aspect of the use of tongues, Fr. Simon Tugwell,O.P. in his book "Did you receive the Spirit?" has this to say:

"In fact, praying in tongues is a weapon of war against

the devil, and against our passions, precisely because it is a prayer of praise, a prayer of peace. God's peace is already established; in praise we assert it against all that is not peace. ' You have established praise ...to destroy the enemy and the avenger' (Psalm 8 v.3) St.Anthony tells how he once 'praised down' a demonic attack. The battle is won in Christ and it is our faith that makes real his victory in each particular situation. *Praying in tongues is one act of faith that can very powerfully claim this victory and establish it effectively, whatever our need may be at the time."*

Tongues opens our hearts to God's Word

The gift of tongues is also a means by which the Holy Spirit opens our hearts and minds to what God is saying to us *now* through His word in scripture. If, to take an example, we are praying scripture in the manner known as lectio divina, we can begin by praying in tongues asking the Holy Spirit to open our hearts to what He wishes to say to us in the scripture we are about to read. As we then begin to read, when a particular verse or phrase of scripture speaks deeply to us, we stop reading and repeat the verse or phrase slowly, aloud, over and over, savouring it, and allowing it to feed us. When we come to our own prayer response, we can then pray in our own language and again go on to pray in tongues. What we find when we do this is that the whole impact of the word we are praying on, and its meaning for us right now, is deepened considerably. The Holy Spirit opens up our hearts to understand and receive the word into fertile soil so that it takes root in us.

Tongues sharpens our awareness of the presence of the Holy Spirit

"I shall ask the Father,
and he will give you another Advocate
to be with you forever,
that Spirit of truth
whom the world can never receive
since it neither sees nor knows him;
but you know him,
because he is with you, he is in you."
(John 14:16-17)

I have come to appreciate over the years that, if we are not careful, we may still vaguely harbour a trace of our old self's mindset, namely, of thinking almighty God is at times very distant from us. After all, we used to sing: "Come Holy Ghost, creator come, *from thy bright heavenly throne...*" Now that sounds quite some distance away, whereas Jesus tells us here in John 14 that the Father will send us 'another "paracletos"' meaning 'another one' - like Jesus Himself who is (literally translating 'paracletos') "one who is called to come to our aid - *to stand by us*" as our *personal helper*.

So it is vital that we grow in the simple awareness of the presence of the Holy Spirit in our personal lives. As we use the gift of tongues more and more, that awareness is sharpened, helping us to be in constant, direct touch with the Holy Spirit, immersed in His love and power and raising everything up with Him to Jesus and the Father.

A key to other gifts of the Spirit

The last purpose I wish to address here is that, in addition to tongues being a gift that is central to our growing in holiness, it also acts as a '*key*' to open us up to the power of the Holy Spirit working in *other* gifts which He may wish to manifest in us from time to time.

As we shall see in the next chapter, when you yield to the gift of tongues, you make a very real, concrete act of faith in the presence of the Holy Spirit within you - physically surrendering your power of speech to Him for His purposes. Make no mistake, this stepping out in faith is of the very same nature as the act of faith that Peter demonstrated when he stepped out of the boat onto the waters of the Sea of Galilee and found the water solid beneath his feet! Through this active trust and faith in the Holy Spirit, *you directly experience the Spirit working through you in power.* And once you have experienced the Holy Spirit working in this way, and seen the fruit of your faith in Him, you become much more sensitive to the prompting of the Holy Spirit within you and more freely allow Him to manifest His other gifts in you.

In this way, the gift of tongues can be seen to be a special key to the operation of other gifts of the Spirit, similar we might say to the way oil helps the moving parts of a machine to operate smoothly.

Perhaps the most obvious illustration of this would be the operation of the gift of prophecy. It is common experience at charismatic prayer meetings for the gathering to be praying in tongues when the Holy Spirit brings everyone to an anointed silence. At that point, the Spirit begins to manifest His gift of prophecy, speaking prophetically (i.e. God's word to those assembled) through various members of the group. In this way, the Holy Spirit not only raises everyone up in praise to Jesus and the Father, but in so doing also opens their hearts to receive His prophetic word. There are other illustrations one could give. The gift of tongues is used extensively, for example, by those involved in exercising the ministries of healing and deliverance, opening themselves to the manifestation of the gifts of knowledge, faith, discernment of spirits and miracles.

I should emphasise here, however, that this is *not* to say that the Holy spirit is in any way unable to manifest His gifts in someone unless they have yielded to the gift of tongues.

FIVE

HOW DO I YIELD TO THE GIFT OF TONGUES?

Tongues is, uniquely, 'there for the asking'

IN THE LIGHT of Cardinal Suenens' teaching that 'the gifts become operative with the job', it is reasonable to ask: 'How can we be confident in coming before the Holy Spirit right now and asking Him to help us to yield to Him and allow Him to pray through us?' Or in other words: 'What job is the Father now entrusting to us for which this gift is to become operative?' The answer is that the gift of tongues is a special gift of *prayer* and the job for which it is manifest is the job every one of us is given the moment we are baptised - namely, the permanent, all embracing job of being witnesses to Christ.

We cannot live our new life in Christ and witness to Him effectively save in the power of the Holy Spirit and growing closer to Jesus each day in prayer. That is why *the gift of tongues is available to everyone for the asking*. In this respect it is unique. Whatever *other* gifts the Holy Spirit may wish to manifest in me will depend on His choosing, at a particular time, and for a particular work entrusted to me. And by way of further contrast with all the other gifts, the gift of tongues is what might be described as a *permanent* gift, in that it is *exercisable by us at will*, whenever we choose. No other gift of the Spirit is exercisable at will in this way, but only as He chooses.

Opening to the gift

So how do we open to this wonderful gift? There are three simple steps to yielding to the gift of tongues:

1. Ask
Come in prayer before the Holy Spirit and simply ask Him to help you yield your voice to Him and allow Him to pray in you. Then move into silence.

2. Expect
Wait silently, in the quietness of your heart, in expectation of the Holy Spirit's response to you. It may help during this waiting time to focus on Jesus in your imagination. Silence is, however, essential.

This is *not* the time to pray the 'Hail Mary' or the 'Glory be', 'Alleluia' or any other form of vocal prayer to give yourself a kind of 'push start'! So long as you persist in praying in *your own* language you are in effect precluding the Holy Spirit from doing the very thing you have asked Him, namely, to pray through you in *His* language. The Spirit will not turn a 'Glory Be' into His new language for you. He requires you to surrender your faculty of speech over to Him so that He can pray through you. So remaining quietly attentive to Him is very important at this time.

3. When prompted, speak out!
As and when you feel a physical urging or prompting by the Holy Spirit to speak out, just do so. Just surrender your speech to Him allowing your tongue and your lips to move and making sound with your voice - but not in your natural language.

You may, however, find that you are not even conscious of any inner prompting and just speak out in tongues spontaneously as the Holy Spirit moves in you. This is a very common experience when people first come into tongues.

The moment the Holy Spirit moves in you to speak out, you will be praying in your own unique language of tongues.

If there is someone praying alongside you in support

at this time, they may suggest that as soon as you feel urged by the Spirit to speak out, you should just do so - *trying to imitate their tongues*. This can be a very effective 'trigger'. You will not manage to imitate them but as soon as you try you will be immediately praying in your own tongue. If this approach is adopted, however, it is important that those praying with you do so at a reasonable speed and do not slow down or over-articulate so that you *can* imitate them!

The following further points should be noted on yielding to this gift:

• Forget any image you may have of swooning saints! Despite the terms used in some scripture translations, the gift of tongues does not induce a state of ecstasy!

• The Holy Spirit's prompting to speak out is unmistakable. Do not resist Him, just surrender your voice to Him.

• When you first pray in tongues, you make an act of faith in opening your mouth and speaking out, just as Peter did when he walked on the water in response to Jesus' bidding. The Holy Spirit will not *force* you to allow Him to speak through you.

• The exercise of the gift of tongues is entirely within your control, to start and stop whenever you want.

What if I don't yield to the gift when I have asked the Holy Spirit to help me?

For a variety of reasons some people do not yield to the gift of tongues as quickly as others. If within four or five minutes you have not prayed out spontaneously in tongues or sensed an inner prompting of the Holy Spirit to do so, do not allow yourself to become frustrated and anxious, waiting on the Holy Spirit. The important thing is that *you have made the decision and invited the Holy Spirit to pray in you.* Just stick to that decision and maintain your desire and attitude of openness.

It is a good idea to take the next opportunity (soon) - when you are fresh - to wait again on the Holy Spirit quietly and expectantly, though again only for a short while. This may be either alone or with some Christian friends praying in tongues in support of you. In coming back to the Holy Spirit faithfully from time to time in prayer in this way, many people find that they come into tongues a few hours or some days later, quite spontaneously, without expecting it.

It is most important, however, that you do not worry if you are not praying in tongues. We can be sure that countess saints down the centuries never prayed in tongues but that did not impede their growing in holiness one iota!

Once I have begun to pray in tongues...

Once you have begun to exercise the gift of tongues, it is important to note the following:-

You can pray in tongues whenever you choose.
Once you have yielded to this gift, you no longer have to wait for any physical urging or prompting from the Holy Spirit in order to pray in tongues. You can then pray in tongues whenever you choose to do so.

Do not give way to any doubting that you are praying in tongues.
Initially, you may experience some doubting as to whether or not you are really praying in tongues and this doubting can result in your being tempted to abandon the use of this crucial gift. Bear in mind that, prior to your praying in tongues, almost all your prayer spoken aloud will have been conceptual prayer controlled by your mind. It is not surprising, therefore, that you may initially find yourself allowing your mind to wander while you are praying in tongues, trying to analyse what you are

saying and 'finding fault' with it, so to speak.

To discourage this, I recommend that you push any such analysing and doubting gently but firmly aside, whenever – and as soon as - you find your mind wandering in this way. Focus not on what you are saying, but on the Lord. To do this, many find it very helpful to hold an image of Jesus in their imagination, or to pray before a favourite icon or picture such as the Divine Mercy. In addition, remind yourself that you have submitted your faculty of speech to the Holy Spirit to permit Him to pray through you, and re-affirm your trust that He is doing so.

Do not compare your tongues with the tongues of others.

Another source of doubting lies in the mistake of comparing your tongues with the tongues of others. Everyone's tongues is unique to them *and the language of tongues varies enormously!* The complexity, or simplicity, of sounds in tongues is not in any way equivalent to the extent of a person's vocabulary in a human language. So, *on no account should you be tempted to doubt you are praying in tongues if they happen to consist of relatively few syllables.* Most people pray in tongues with very simple, repetitive sounds and syllables and *however* simple your tongues seem to be, remember it is the Holy Spirit Himself who is praying in you. Ask the Holy Spirit to help you learn to focus your heart and mind on the Lord when you are praying in tongues and allow Him full rein to pray in you in whatever way He chooses.

Get your tongues 'confirmed'

If you are alone when you yield to this gift, or are troubled by doubts as to its being 'genuine', it is helpful to pray in tongues along with someone else also exercising this gift and ask them to confirm to you whether or not you are truly praying in the Spirit. Anyone with maturity in the Spirit and praying in tongues is able to discern this immediately and confirm it to you, because the Spirit praying in them will pick up the reverberations of the Spirit praying in you. Once you have received confirmation that you are praying in tongues, you should place complete reliance on it. Such confirmation will then prevent the distraction of doubts from developing or continuing.

Persevere!

As to perseverance, when people first begin to pray in tongues it is quite common for them to pray at length, even for hours at a time! However, when the 'novelty' of this experience wears off, it is quite astonishing how many end up praying only occasionally in tongues, or even not bothering to pray in tongues at all! *This is a **disaster**!!*

When you think for a moment of how magnificently this gift builds us up in our relationship with the Lord, in our openness to the movement of the Holy Spirit in our lives, and in our power to witness to the saving love of Jesus, the saddest thing is to allow it to fall into abeyance. To do so also disarms you of one of your most powerful weapons in the spiritual battle in which we are all engaged. The answer to this is to persevere, *come what may*, in using the gift of tongues *every day* in your prayer.

While, of course, the whole discipline of prayer needs to be built up and it is counter-productive to set targets we cannot reasonably meet, I would urge you to pray in tongues initially for five to ten minutes each day *at the very least*, and allow this to increase as the Holy Spirit increases your hunger and capacity for this most powerful form of prayer.

One of the best ways of developing your use of tongues is to make a practice of 'weaving' tongues into your 'ordinary' prayers. For example, if you are praying the rosary, begin at the outset by asking the Holy Spirit to open your heart to the various mysteries you will be contemplating, and then pray in tongues for a minute or so. As you spend a little time contemplating the mystery before each decade, again move into tongues just for a minute or so. Similarly, when you pray the 'Our Father', it is easy to intersperse tongues between each element of it: "Our Father, who art in heaven, hallowed be thy name…tongues…thy kingdom come…tongues…thy will be done on earth as it is in heaven…tongues… etc.

I would also strongly recommend you use tongues when you are praying the psalms. As you pray a psalm (ideally aloud) intersperse tongues between each stanza of the psalm: stanza…tongues…stanza… tongues…etc. As you pray in tongues in this way, the Holy Spirit will open up the psalm to speak more and more deeply to you.

As you use tongues in your prayer in this way, you will find praying in tongues becomes second nature to you, as easy as breathing, and you will learn to pray in tongues more and more throughout your day.

Apart from the supreme example of St.Paul himself, one of the best examples of the importance of persevering with praying in tongues is given by Jackie Pullinger in her book 'Chasing the Dragon'. In that book she recounts her great adventure in going to Hong Kong and bringing the gospel to the Triad gangsters in the walled city. She mentions that when she first arrived, nothing much seemed to happen, and it was then that she decided to pray in tongues every day "*...fifteen minutes by the clock!...*" When she started to do that, the Holy Spirit began to move powerfully and the gang members began to surrender their lives to Jesus.

It is clear from this account that Jackie was led to adopt the discipline of praying in tongues for quarter of an hour each day – with spectacular results! It is also worth mentioning, too, that *every single one* of the Triad gang members that have been brought to Jesus through Jackie's ministry were helped to come into the gift of tongues. This is very strong testimony to my understanding that the gift is indeed available to everyone. Finally, at the end of her book, Jackie mentions that she prays more or less constantly in tongues throughout her day, rather as I imagine St.Paul himself did.

APPENDIX ONE

ANSWERS TO QUESTIONS COMMONLY ASKED

Question 1
Does the gift of tongues render prayer in my natural language a 'second rate' form of prayer?

Answer
Not in the slightest. All prayer comes from the action of the Holy Spirit within us, and it is important *not* to view prayer in our natural language as in any way 'inferior' to praying in tongues. We have the example of Jesus teaching his disciples to pray what is described as the greatest prayer - the 'Our Father' - and there was never any suggestion from Jesus that tongues would somehow supersede the use of that prayer.

In introducing the 'Our Father', we also have Jesus encouraging us to keep our prayers simple:
"In your prayers do not babble as the pagans do, for they think that by using many words they will make themselves heard. Do not be like them; your Father knows what you need before you ask him." (Matthew 6:7-9)

The gift of tongues has to be understood as supplement-ing prayer in our natural language, and particularly when our natural language begins to fail us, or fails us completely.

Question 2
How do I curb my tendency to analyse my tongues when I am praying?

Answer
When you first begin to pray in tongues, this tendency to analyse what you are saying is very common and can be quite distracting. It can be difficult for the brain to be kept 'in neutral', so to speak, while you are praying in tongues – not least perhaps because your brain has in the past been fully engaged in your conceptual prayer. The best remedy is to give your mind something to focus on, either by way of keeping an image of Jesus in your mind as you pray, or by praying (for example) before a favourite icon. This will keep your attention off what you are saying, and your focus on the Lord.

Sometimes the tendency may arise from an underlying doubt as to whether or not you are really praying in tongues, and can even itself give rise to such doubting. If that is the case either way, it is important to dispel such doubting once and for all by getting your tongues 'confirmed' - see Chapter Five.

Question 3
Is this gift meant to be used principally in one's private prayer time?

Answer
I think this question often arises out of a mis-understanding that in 1 Corinthians 14 St.Paul is discouraging us from using tongues in public. (For further on this, see Question 4 in Appendix 2.) Chapter 14 is addressing the use of tongues in *public worship* i.e. a formal and public gathering of members of the Church. He is not addressing the use of tongues in the informal gathering of a prayer group, where the gift of tongues is rightly used extensively.

Having said all that, while tongues is not in any way meant to be *confined* to private prayer, in practice – if we allow this gift to grow in the way we should - it is likely that we will pray in tongues much more on our own than with other people.

Question 4

I think I once prayed in tongues (many years ago) but have never done so since. How do I know if I prayed in tongues and can I revive this gift?

Answer

Sadly, this is a very common occurrence largely due to lack of receiving confirmation when people first pray in tongues, that they are doing so. I have prayed with literally hundreds of people who have had a similar story. My practice has been to ask them to join with me in praying in tongues so that I can give them confirmation of whether or not they are praying in tongues as well. So my advice to you is to do the same: ask for confirmation of your tongues just as soon as you can from someone who prays in tongues.

As to reviving the gift, once you have prayed in tongues, you can always pray in tongues, so reviving this gift simply amounts to using it again.

I am pleased to tell you that I cannot remember a single case in which someone who has shared this problem with me had not in fact prayed in tongues.

Question 5
Why do some people take longer than others to yield to the gift of tongues?

Answer
I think there is a variety of reasons why some take longer than others to yield to the gift of tongues. Over the years, I have come to the conclusion that in the vast majority of cases it seems most unlikely to reflect the Spirit's timetable, but rather the person being very self conscious and physically holding back – reluctant to take that small step of faith in speaking out.

In other cases, poor self image, a feeling of unworthiness, or a feeling of guilt over past sins, can result in some people in effect resisting the Spirit for a while, thinking that He will not want to pray in them – when, of course, the very opposite is in fact the case.

If you do not yield to the gift of tongues initially once you have asked, avoid thinking you must have some kind of unidentified 'block' that will have to be cleared first and, above all, do not worry that you are not praying in tongues.

Question 6
How do you sing in tongues?

Answer

I think most people find it easier to pray in tongues than to sing in tongues. Having said that, you sing in tongues in exactly the same way as you pray in tongues, by surrendering your voice in song to the Holy Spirit as He may prompt you. When you do this, you are not giving Him the melody: He is giving *you* the melody!

The reason I emphasise that is because it is my firm impression that in many gatherings there are numbers of people who are not *really* allowing the Holy Spirit full freedom to sing in them. Instead they are cautiously 'lalala – ing' and trying consciously to keep in harmony with those nearby. If that is the case, then they are not really singing in the Spirit. By contrast, when a large gathering of people fully surrender their singing voices to the Spirit, He composes the most amazing symphony embracing all kinds of sound (including dissonant notes) which those gifted in music composition find quite staggering in its complexity and beauty.

Here I would put in a special plea to those engaged in music ministry. Certainly at major conferences they almost invariably introduce an opportunity for singing in the Spirit by holding down some loud, basic chords. I am sure they believe this is helpful in 'giving a lead' and possibly 'giving cover' to everyone wishing to sing out. However, if you reflect on that, it is like giving the Holy Spirit a couple of chords and inviting Him to use them as the base sound for *His* song! The plain fact is, He has plenty of chords of His own. In these circumstances, therefore, in order to sing really freely in tongues you desperately try to ignore the music, which is more than most of us can manage. The result in practice is that almost everyone is *railroaded into singing a melody in C*, rather than singing in the Spirit! Now there is nothing wrong in singing a melody in C to the Lord – St.Paul actually encourages us to do so (Ephesians 5: 19). But if we want to sing *in tongues*, the music ministry should simply sing out in tongues when they feel led by the Holy Spirit to do so - without any instrumental accompaniment - thereby inviting everyone to join with them. In that way the Spirit can be given full rein to compose exactly what He wishes.

Some people, when they are first opening their hearts to yield to the Holy Spirit in tongues, find it difficult to just wait for the action or prompting of the Spirit and consciously 'default' into 'making a melody' for

the Lord. Now, it is fine to make a melody for the
Lord, but if *you* are making the melody and not the
Holy Spirit, then you are not singing in tongues. This
has to be watched out for when you are encouraging
someone to yield to the gift.

Question 7
**Some people say they can *only* sing in tongues –
and cannot pray in tongues. Can you comment on
that?**

Answer
As a preliminary point, it is worth noting that some
people do sing out in tongues spontaneously when
they first come into the gift of tongues, but in my
personal experience this has been comparatively
rare.

Just occasionally, I have come across people who
have told me that they can sing in tongues but cannot
pray in tongues. My practice has been to reassure
them that if they are truly singing in the Spirit (and
that needs to be confirmed), then there is no doubt
that they can also pray in the Spirit. And I encourage
them to do so.

Question 8
Do you lose the gift of tongues if you don't use it?

Answer

In the 1970s, the early years of the renewal in the Catholic Church, it was common to hear people say: "If you don't use it, you'll lose it." Most unfortunately, this remark carries the awful connotation that if you do not use the gift of tongues, then God will take it away from you! Nothing could be further, of course, from God's nature, and we have His word in scripture that He never takes back what He has given: "God never takes back His gifts or revokes His choice." (Romans 11:29) So it is beyond doubt that the Holy Spirit always remains ready to pray in you.

The truth is, however, that if you do not persevere in praying in tongues and allow the gift to flourish in the way it is meant to, then it is easy for it to fall into abeyance, even to the point of your no longer praying in tongues at all. In this way the gift has not been 'lost' (i.e. you could still pray in tongues if you wanted to) but has sadly fallen into total abeyance. That is something to avoid at all costs.

Question 9
Can tongues change?

Answer
Over a period of time many people's tongues do
change, perhaps in some cases because they are
surrendering themselves more fully to the Holy
Spirit. However, it is very important not to allow
yourself to become distracted by focussing on what
you are saying when you pray in tongues. Keep your
heart and mind focussed on the Lord and let the
Holy Spirit have full rein to pray in you in whatever
way he wishes.

Question 10
**Are very young children capable of praying in
tongues?**

Answer
Yes. I happen to have come across two cases in
schools where whole classes of children around the
ages of 9 and 10 all exercised the gift of tongues. The
youngest child I have personally met who prayed in
tongues was three. To confirm for her mother that
her child was indeed praying in tongues, I asked the
child if she would pray along with me in her 'special'

language and she prayed in tongues very fluently
with me for several minutes.

Question 11

**How would I know if I am speaking out in a tongue
prophetically - will my tongues be different in that
case?**

Answer

I cannot say that when someone speaks in tongues
prophetically their tongues are *always* different
from how they pray in tongues, but I know that it is
often the case. Furthermore, if the person speaking
recognises a change in their tongues and thinks
they may be speaking prophetically, it is very helpful
if they simply say so at the end: '...I believe this may
be a word of prophecy.' Notice I use the term '*may
be*'. It is for the gathering to discern whether or not
it is in fact a word of prophecy.

Question 12

**How do you know if someone else speaking out in
tongues is speaking prophetically?**

Answer

First of all, the manifestation of the gift of
discernment will identify whether or not the Holy
Spirit *is* speaking through someone. But in any
event, if someone is speaking a prophecy in tongues,
then the Holy Spirit is *certainly* going to give the
interpretation to the group. Without interpretation,
there would be no point in a prophecy being given
in tongues – it would just remain unintelligible. So,
whenever anyone does speak out (i.e. on their own)
in tongues, unless someone discerns it is not
prophetic and says so, the whole group should pray
for an interpretation and they should *all* be open to
the Spirit to give it.

Question 13
**Can the Holy Spirit pray in me in more than one
tongue?**

Answer

Yes. Some people do have a variety of tongues, just
as some of the disciples did in the early Church.
However, these are not normally *prayer* tongues. It
is quite common, for example, for people exercising
deliverance ministry, in the course of which they will
be praying extensively in their 'usual' tongue, to use

a different tongue when *commanding* demonic spirits to leave. Likewise, those who speak a word of *prophecy* in tongues often speak out in a tongue which is different from the tongue they normally pray in.

I have come across people who actually *pray* in a variety of tongues, but this is not a common experience by any means. Whatever you do, do not get hung up on wondering if you may yet experience another type of tongues! Just get busy praying in the tongues you have! If at some stage the Holy Spirit wants to pray in you in a totally different way, then it will just happen.

Question 14
Can you pray in tongues 'silently' – just thinking of words in your mind?

Answer
It might be helpful to mention here that in some cases when people first yield to the gift of tongues they initially experience some form of 'words' coming into their minds, coupled with an inner urging from the Holy Spirit to speak them out.

Now, turning to the question: first of all, you cannot come into the gift of tongues unless you actually surrender your voice, praying aloud as the Holy Spirit moves in you. There is no question of the Spirit operating some kind of 'silent' equivalent!

If you already exercise the gift of tongues, you might possibly be able to give expression in your mind to some simple sounds or syllables that actually form part of your tongues language and who am I to discount that as prayer? However, I think it is fair to say that the normal exercise of this gift is in oral, vocalised prayer, and anyone praying in tongues can, if they wish, do so discreetly by praying very softly under their breath, so no-one would be even aware they were praying in this way.

Question 15
Why did the use of tongues die out in the Church?

Answer
The short answer to this question is that the use of tongues did not die out altogether in the Church. Many of the saints over the centuries are recorded as using the gift of tongues. It is also the case that tongues has formed part of the monastic prayer

tradition in Russia for well over a thousand years - ever since Russia was converted. It is true, however, that the use of tongues otherwise - within the general body of the Church - appears to have largely died out and it is something of a mystery that it did so. Today we find the very opposite, with the Holy Spirit manifesting this gift as part of His huge outpouring all over the world – in preparation for the return of Jesus.

Question 16
Can you say something more about tongues and spiritual warfare?

Answer
Well, the first point I would make is that in coping with temptation the watchword (for which I am indebted to Fr. Pat Collins, C.M.) is: "Don't wrestle – nestle!" In other words, we are on a slippery slope once we start wrestling with temptation. So don't get into the fight – just nestle in the protection of the precious wounds of Jesus! And by far the best possible way of doing that (as mentioned in Chapter 4) is to pray in tongues.

We should also all be aware that St.Alphonsus

exhorted every Christian to exercise the power they
had to command any demonic spirit that they may
sense is troubling them to depart. The following is a
prayer based on the prayer for use by the laity that
he advocated:

"Evil spirit, in the name of Jesus Christ I command
you to depart from me and no longer trouble me, and
I send you to Jesus to be dealt with as He wills. You
are not to trouble anyone or anything else on the face
of the earth. Begone!"

This is a prayer of *command*. You are not *asking* the
evil spirit to stop bothering you: you are *commanding*
him to stop and go away. So the prayer should be
spoken with confidence and faith that you speak
with the authority of Jesus Himself. I recommend
that you pray in tongues for protection beforehand
and speak out in tongues afterwards *by way of
reinforcement of your command*. Tongues is utterly
repellant to evil spirits: they cannot bear to hear
tongues being spoken. Finally, end this time of
prayer by praying in tongues, asking the Holy Spirit
to minister His peace and healing to you.

Question 17

How does praying in tongues contrast with the eastern practice of using a mantra?

Answer

The language of mantras is entirely different from the gift of tongues. Mantras are phrases in human language generally taken from Hindu hymns and used as an aid to concentration and with the intention of developing spiritual power.

The contrast with tongues could hardly be sharper. Tongues is an unknown language of love given to us directly by the Holy Spirit in which we are one with the mind and heart of the living God. Forget mantras – use tongues!

Question 18

Can you comment further on how the gift of tongues was manifest at Pentecost?

Answer

The account which Paul went on to give to the other apostles in Jerusalem of the conversion of Cornelius and his household sheds a very interesting light on what probably happened in the upper room and immediately afterwards on the streets of Jerusalem. We read in Acts 11:15 as follows:-

"I had scarcely begun to speak when the Holy Spirit came down on them *in the same way as it came down on us at the beginning....*"

Now in the case of Cornelius' household, they all spoke out in tongues in the normal way i.e. each in an unknown language. There was no need whatsoever for the Holy Spirit to be speaking in them any known, human languages because they all spoke the same native language. It can then be reasonably argued from this that when the Holy Spirit came down on everyone in the upper room, they all spoke *at first* in tongues *in the normal way* (because, as with Cornelius' household, those gathered in the upper room all spoke the same native language). It was only when they began to preach to the crowds of other races in Jerusalem that the Holy Spirit either then spoke through them in all the various languages represented there, or they continued to speak in tongues in the normal way, with the Holy Spirit anointing the listeners so that each could hear them in their own language.

ANSWERS TO QUESTIONS COMMONLY ARISING ON THE INTERPRETATION OF 1 CORINTHIANS 12 & 14

THERE ARE a number of misunderstandings, unfortunately quite prevalent, concerning how the Holy Spirit works in us and also the use of tongues, some of which arise out of the mistranslation or misinterpretation of what St.Paul says in chapters 12 and 14 of his first letter to the Corinthians.

Question 1
1 Cor.12:7 reads in the Jerusalem Bible:-
"The particular way in which the Spirit is *given to each person* is for a good purpose."
This seems to say quite clearly that gifts *are* given to everyone – in contradiction of what Cardinal Suenens teaches, and that, perhaps, each of us has only one, special gift. How do you reconcile this conflict?

Answer
I am delighted to say that the problem here is not

one of contradiction, but of mistranslation. The use of the word "*given*" in this particular translation is most unfortunate. The literal translation of the Greek text in verse 7 reads: "the *manifestation* of the Spirit given to each individual..." and the sense of the passage is best captured by the Revised English Bible which renders it: "In each of us the Spirit *is seen to be at work* for some useful purpose."

So, the correct overview of what Paul is saying in 1 Cor. 12:4-11 is that there is a great variety of ways in which the Holy Spirit is at work in his gifts (of which Paul goes on to give a number of examples) and that whatever gift the Spirit *may be manifesting in a particular person at any particular time* is manifest for the common good. In this way the whole body is empowered by the Holy Spirit to serve the body of Christ and the proclamation of the gospel.

It is worth noting, too, just for the sake of completeness, that Paul could not possibly be interpreted as indicating that the Holy Spirit will only manifest in each of us one special gift when – for example - he goes on to encourage everyone to be eager for the higher gifts and especially the gift of prophecy. (See 1 Cor.12: 31 and 14:1).

One has only to reflect, too, on the fact that St.Paul himself is recorded as experiencing the manifestation of a whole range of the gifts of the Holy Spirit – including (to name but a few!) healing, tongues, miracles, faith, deliverance, discernment, leadership, teaching, preaching, and prophecy - to recognise that he is calling us to be open to whatever way the Holy spirit may wish to use us at any particular time.

Question 2

1 Cor.12:27 – 30 reads:-

"Now you together are Christ's body; but each of you is a different part of it. In the Church, God has given first place to apostles, the second to prophets, the third to teachers...." and goes on to mention others, including "those with many languages". And Paul continues with the rhetorical question: "Are all of them apostles, or all of them prophets... do all speak in tongues?" to which the answer understood is 'No'.

You maintain that the gift of tongues is available to everyone, but doesn't this text clearly say that not everyone can speak in tongues?

Answer

Just as a preliminary point, I need to say that while the gift of tongues is available to us, I am not maintaining that everyone 'should' or 'must' pray in tongues. There is no 'should' or 'must' about it. Now, to go back to your question, the short answer is 'No'. The point here is that verses 27-30 are about *ministries* as distinct from gifts. A *ministry* arises when a gift is manifested in someone on such a regular basis that the community discerns they have a special calling to be used in that particular gift. To illustrate the distinction, everyone may from time to time pray for somebody's healing, but not everyone will be called to work in healing ministry. Similarly, many people will be given a prophetic word, but only a few will be called to serve the community by way of a dedicated prophetic ministry.

To go back to the text, what is very interesting here is that verse 30 says: 'Do all speak strange languages'. Now the Greek phrase used for 'speaking in tongues' is exactly the same as the phrase used for 'speaking in strange (or foreign) languages.' Furthermore, the Greek used for 'tongues' is sometimes in the singular ('a tongue') and sometimes in the plural ('tongues') usually without intending any distinction between the two. All of this makes things difficult for

translators! However, in the case of verse 30, it is
clear that the plural *is* intended and Paul is saying:
"Do all speak in various different tongues?" What is
puzzling, however, is that this must mean that there
were some within the community who exercised
some kind of ministry through the use of a variety
of tongues and we are given no further indication
of exactly what that ministry entailed. I think it is
possible that the variety of tongues might have
embraced actual known human languages, but that
is pure conjecture on my part.

Question 3
**Is Paul speaking disparagingly of tongues when
he says: "Be ambitious for the *higher* gifts."
(1 Cor.12:31)?**

Answer
No. This is a very common misunderstanding which
I should like to lay to rest. Some regard this sentence
as indicating that Paul thought the gift of tongues
was not such an important gift, even '*the least*' of the
gifts. However, this is a serious misunderstanding.
All that Paul is stressing here, and elsewhere in
Chapter 14, is that while he wants everyone to use
their gift of tongues, they should not 'rest on their

laurels', so to speak. They must allow the Holy Spirit to move further in them and be open to the other gifts which He will undoubtedly wish to manifest, *particularly* the gift of prophecy.

And while on this subject concerning Paul's attitude to the gift of tongues, Paul's own constant use of tongues (evidenced in 1.Cor.14:18) is enough to demonstrate just how vitally important Paul regarded this gift. Nor should we overlook the force of his concluding remarks in 1 Cor. 14:39-40: "And so, my dear brothers, by all means be ambitious to prophesy, *do not suppress the gift of tongues,* but let everything be done with propriety and in order."

Question 4
In 1 Cor.14:27 we read:-
"If any speak in a tongue, let there be only two or at the most three, and each in turn; and let one interpret." (RSV)
This restriction seems to show that Paul strongly discourages the use of the gift of tongues when we meet to pray together and that it should be mainly confined to private use. Is that understanding correct?

Answer

No. It is a total misunderstanding. The first point to make here is that in Chapter 14 Paul is giving the Corinthians instructions concerning the use of tongues in *public worship* – which is open to non-believers. He explains that in those circumstances it is unhelpful to non-believers present if they all just pray aloud in tongues praising and thanking God. If they do that, non-believers will not understand a word they are saying and will think they have taken leave of their senses (v23)! Furthermore, and much more important, he points out that they will be missing a golden opportunity to proclaim the prophetic word from the Holy Spirit which will speak deeply to the unbelievers in their presence.

Turning to verse 27 itself, the point to note here is that Paul is *not* talking in this verse about people *praying* in tongues, but *speaking out* in tongues - *in prophecy!* - hence the all important phrase at the end: 'and let one *interpret*.'

Finally, it is worth keeping in mind that Paul's injunction here could never possibly be taken as a general 'all time' ban applicable to church gatherings, no more than his ban on women speaking (verse 34) can be so interpreted!

Question 5

In the Jerusalem Bible translation of 1 Cor.14:5 we read: "While I should like you all to have the gift of tongues, I would much rather you could prophesy..."

Paul's remarks here seem rather disjointed. Can you please comment generally on the translation and interpretation of this text?

Answer

Indeed, I agree with what you have said. Interestingly there is another possible translation of verse 5 which, following the literal translation of the Greek, would read: *'Now I want you all to pray in tongues'* (i.e. 'Now I want you all to *use* your gift of tongues'). And instead of the text going on to read: 'I would much rather you could prophesy', the Greek could also be translated: 'but rather *so that* you would prophesy.' In other words, Paul is encouraging everyone to pray in tongues *in order to receive whatever prophetic word the Holy Spirit may wish to give them* – rather than just going on and on praying aloud in tongues.

*Further copies of this book
can be obtained from*

Goodnews Books
*upper level car park
St. John the Apostle Church
296 Sundon Park Road
Luton, Beds. LU3 3AL*

*www.goodnewsbooks.net
orders@goodnewsbooks.net
01582 571011*